The Day the Energies Saved the World

By Candice Lemon-Scott

Illustrated by Marc Lynch

Pearson Australia
(a division of Pearson Australia Group Pty Ltd)
707 Collins Street, Melbourne, Victoria 3008
PO Box 23360, Melbourne, Victoria 8012
www.pearson.com.au

First published 2014 by Pearson Australia
2021 2020 2019 2018
10 9 8 7 6 5 4 3 2 1

Publisher: Kieren Noonan
Project Managers: Tamara Pirois and Rachel Davis
Lead Editor: Kerry Nagle
Editor: Sally Green
Cover and series designer: Jenny Grigg
Designers: Jennifer Johnston and Nina Heryanto
Copyright & Pictures Editor: Julia Weaver
Mac Operator: Rob Curulli
Cover art: Marc Lynch
Illustrator: Marc Lynch
Printed in Australia by the SOS Print + Media Group

ISBN 978 1 4860 0749 3

Pearson Australia Group Pty Ltd ABN 40 004 245 943

Disclaimer
Some of the images used in *The Day the Energies Saved the World* might have associations with deceased Indigenous Australians. Please be aware that these images might cause sadness or distress in Aboriginal or Torres Strait Islander communities.

Contents

ALERT ISSUED: CODE STW

CURRENT STATUS: 10 per cent liquid iron left

RESULT: Earth to stop spinning in 48 hours

YOUR MISSION: Stop liquid iron removal on the other side of the Earth

THE ENERGIES TEAM:

Hydro

Solar

Wind

Report to Energy Station One immediately.
The fate of the world is in your hands.

Ms X

Chapter 1

The mission

Ms X, the head of EarthGuard Centre, hit the send button. The letter was sent to the three children: Hydro, Solar and Wind. Next, she called out, "Doctor Rock." Within moments his face appeared on the screen.

"Hello, Ms X," Doctor Rock said in a grumpy voice.

"How are things on the other side of the Earth?" Ms X asked, worried.

"Very bad. The liquid iron meter is very low, there's not much left," he said.

The outer core of the Earth was made of liquid iron. Liquid iron drilling had started twenty years ago as an experiment by a group of scientists looking for a new source of energy.

The scientists used some very hi-tech robots to do the drilling. But a few years ago, some robots came into contact with the liquid iron and things went terribly wrong. They rebelled and took over the mine site. Now there was a whole army of robots, drilling all the liquid iron from the Earth's outer core.

The liquid iron in the outer core made the Earth spin. But too much liquid iron had been taken out and the Earth had almost stopped spinning.

Soon the Earth would stop turning altogether. Instead of having day and night, there would only be darkness on one side, and light on the other.

"I'm sending a team to help you, Doctor Rock. Hopefully Wind, Solar and Hydro can stop the machines."

"I hope so. It will take a lot to stop these machines from drilling. They're huge."

The screen went blank. Ms X hoped they could help, too.

Meanwhile, Wind was staring at the letter from Ms X. He couldn't believe it. STW stood for 'Save the World'. But how could he help? He was just a kid who could make power from the wind.

When Wind was born, a tornado had lifted him and his family into the wind. Being in a tornado had left him with special powers. He was able to create energy using the power of wind.

Now he sat in his teleport seat and sent the computer his destination using his thoughts, *Earth Station One*.

Chapter 2

On the other side

Wind appeared on Earth Station One. It was here that Wind, Hydro and Solar created electricity using their powers. Solar and Hydro also had special powers, like Wind. Solar was born on a space station during a solar flare and could now use the Sun's energy. Hydro's birth was just before a tsunami. A giant wave had picked him and his mother up and set them down two blocks away. Now he had the ability to use the power of water.

"You're finally here, Wind," Ms X said.

"Yes, Ms X," he mumbled.

Wind was surprised to see Hydro and Solar were already there. But then, they were better than him at everything. Wind found out years ago that his talent was the weakest of the three. It wasn't much fun being outshone by kids a year younger than you.

Ms X quickly explained their latest mission. They only had two days to stop the giant drilling machines on the other side of the planet and save the world. Using 3D images of the Earth, she showed them how things were changing. The days and nights were getting longer and longer as liquid iron was removed and the Earth's spin slowed. They also saw the mine site on the other side of the world, where the giant drilling machines were taking out the liquid iron.

She told them that without the balance of day and night, all life on Earth would soon die.

"I need you all to join Doctor Rock at Spy Control Centre on the other side of the Earth. Please be seated."

The three energies sat in the teleport seats. Wind closed his eyes, still wondering how he was supposed to help save the world He felt himself teleport away and opened his eyes.

"Where are we?" Hydro asked.

Just then, a short man appeared. He had long whiskers and an even longer nose. He was staring at them over a pair of thick glasses.

"Ms X has sent me children to save the world? This is terrible!" he cried in horror.

Wind felt himself glowing with anger, "Well, the adults haven't done much good."

"There are only two days until the Earth will stop spinning," the man said. He pointed to a liquid iron meter. It was glowing orange.

The man sat down in front of a computer screen. He brought up an image of the mine site. He shook his head sadly, ignoring the three children. Then he turned to them.

"Since you're here, I guess you'd better come with me. I'm Doctor Rock."

Chapter 3

Battle with the machines

Wind, Solar and Hydro followed Doctor Rock along a long, narrow tunnel. Soon they got to a dead end. Doctor Rock stretched his arms up above his head. He pushed on the rock above him. A hatch opened and bright light streamed in.

"Wow!" Hydro exclaimed.

Doctor Rock pulled down a ladder. He started to climb it. When he got to the top, he waved them up.

"Where are we going?" Wind asked.

"Shhh!" he said. "We have to be quiet as the robots are everywhere in this building. This is where the liquid iron is stored."

Wind, Solar and Hydro climbed the ladder. Doctor Rock gently closed the hatch behind them. They were in a circular room. It was bigger than anything Wind had ever seen. In the middle stood a huge black cylinder.

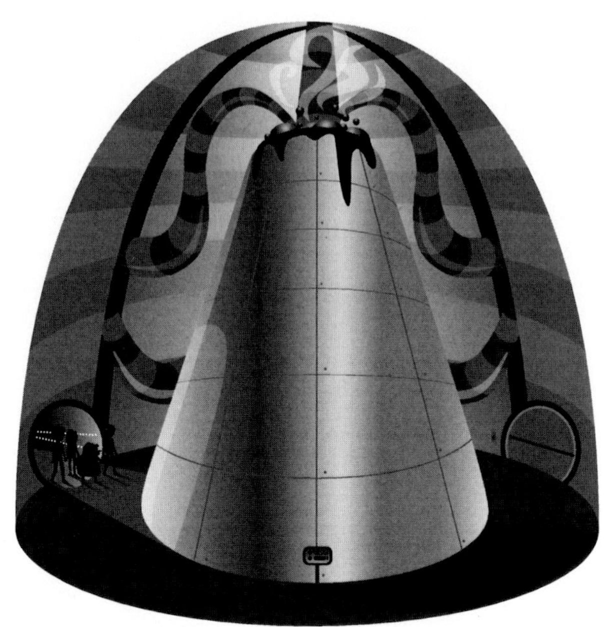

"Liquid iron," Doctor Rock said, pointing to the huge cylinder.

Long, thick pipes led into it at the top. The pipes came in through gaps in the building. Outside somewhere was the mine site. The three followed Doctor Rock around the cylinder until they came to a small, green door. He opened the door slowly and poked his head out.

“It’s all clear,” he said.

The energies followed the doctor into the cold, dark air outside.

Wind wished he had a big, warm jacket on. It was so cold on this side of the planet. Back home it was warm because the Sun was shining. There, the day was lasting for a very long time.

He knew it was only going to get worse though. When all the liquid iron was taken out, the Earth would finally stop spinning. Then back at home they’d be facing the Sun all the time. There’d no longer be day and night. On this side it would be cold and dark. An endless night.

Doctor Rock was heading towards a lit-up area. As the children followed behind, Wind saw it was the mine site. Half the earth had been dug out.

They came to a huge pit that seemed to have no bottom. Massive machines were scattered around the mine site. Each machine had a gigantic drill attached to it.

Wind started to think Doctor Rock had been right. What could three children do against these huge steel monsters?

Just then a robot sitting in a machine's control box sent a drill deep into the Earth's crust. Liquid iron was removed and sent through huge pipes into the power station. Wind watched as the machine moved across the treeless land and disappeared.

"What do they need all that liquid iron for?" Hydro asked.

"It creates electricity for this side of the world using its heat," Doctor Rock whispered.

"But we need liquid iron for the Earth to spin," Solar added.

"Exactly," Doctor Rock agreed.

"What can we do against those massive machines?" Hydro cried. "Not even a wall of water could knock one of them over."

"And I could never make it hot enough to melt that much metal," Solar added.

"Maybe I could blow one over with a wind burst," Wind said, sarcastically.

"No one else has been able to stop the mining," Doctor Rock said, "You are our last hope. It's up to you to destroy the mine!"

Chapter 4

Attack of the robots

The three energies stood behind Doctor Rock. They were in front of one of the great machines. It was so huge that Wind couldn't even see the top of it.

"Who's first?" Doctor Rock asked.

Hydro and Solar looked at Wind.

"Why me?" Wind cried.

"You said your wind energy could topple one of the machines," Hydro said.

"I was just joking," Wind whined.

Hydro and Solar pushed him forward. Wind sucked all the air around him up into an invisible ball of wind. He sent it flying towards the machine. It began to sway. Then … nothing.

"Oh dear!" Doctor Rock said.

"Let me try," Hydro insisted.

Hydro gathered the water from a nearby river up into a ball. He threw the ball of water over the machine and it crashed down like a gigantic waterfall. The machine shifted from side to side. Then … nothing.

"Oh dear!" Doctor Rock said again.

"I guess it's my turn," Solar remarked.

Solar brought the heat of the Sun into her hands and pushed it at the machine. The machine started to catch fire. But then … nothing.

"Now what?" Wind asked.

Suddenly they felt the ground under them shake. They all looked around. An army of robots had formed in neat rows.

"Oh no!" Doctor Rock cried.

A siren rang out. The robots began to move in formation straight towards them.

"Run!" Doctor Rock screamed.

The three children ran across the mine site with Doctor Rock trailing behind.

The sound of the robots' metal feet echoing on the ground became louder and louder. They reached the edge of the mining pit. Wind glanced over his shoulder. The robots were only metres away. There was nowhere else to go. They were trapped.

"We're going to have to fight the robots," Wind exclaimed.

"But there are hundreds of them," Solar moaned.

"It's our only chance," Hydro argued.

Solar took in the Sun's energy, Hydro gathered in the water from the lake and Wind sucked in a gale.

They each sent all the force of the wind, water and Sun straight towards the robots.

First, the robots started toppling with the wind. Then, Hydro sent a rush of water after them and pushed them towards the pit. Solar threw all her Sun energy at them. The robots melted before their eyes.

With one last burst of energy, Wind pushed the melted metal into the pit.

"Amazing!" Doctor Rock cried out. "But we still have work to do. We need more liquid iron in the centre of the Earth to keep our planet spinning."

Chapter 5

Saving the world

The children and Doctor Rock returned to the underground Spy Control Centre.

"We need to think," Doctor Rock said.

“If the Earth stops spinning, the plants on one side will be in the dark. They will die. And on the light side, bees and butterflies won’t pollinate plants without any seasons to guide them. Soon there will be nothing to eat. There’s no time left. Oh, we’re all doomed.”

“There has to be a way,” Wind said.

He looked at the liquid iron meter. Surprisingly, it was now a light orange colour.

“Wait! The liquid iron levels have risen.”

“But there should be less, not more,” Solar exclaimed.

“The robots. They must be made of the liquid iron too,” Hydro added.

“That’s why the level’s gone up on the meter,” Solar squealed excitedly.

“That’s it!” Wind said. “We have to put the liquid iron back into the Earth.”

"How can we do that?" Hydro asked.

"Like we did with the robots. We combine energies. Let's work together one more time!" Wind said to his friends.

"Wind, Solar, Hydro!" the children shouted together, and joined knuckles.

First, Solar had to heat the liquid iron to make it as hot as it had been in the centre of the Earth. She brought in the Sun's energy and pushed it into the cylinder. The liquid iron began to boil and bubble until it was hot enough to return to the Earth.

Hydro took over from there. He had to keep the pipes cool so that the heat of the liquid iron wouldn't melt them as it passed through. He took the water from the nearby rivers and lakes and sent it swirling around the pipes.

It was Wind's turn next. He had to blow the liquid iron through the pipes. If it didn't move quickly enough, the iron would melt the pipes before it reached the centre of the Earth. Wind sent wind energy through the pipes, pushing the liquid iron along until it poured back into the ground.

When they had finished, Doctor Rock and the three energies stared at the liquid iron meter. It was still orange. Maybe they were too late after all.

"You did your best," said Doctor Rock.

Wind looked at the liquid iron meter. Then he noticed the meter was changing colour, to yellow. The liquid iron levels rose even further, turning green.

"Look! They're back at safe levels," Doctor Rock cried.

"It worked!" Solar and Hydro cried.

"What about the machines?" Wind interrupted. "We couldn't topple them. If there are any robots left, they will just start the mining again."

"Leave that to me," Doctor Rock said.

The three children followed him to the surface. At the mine pit the doctor closed his eyes and raised his hands. The edges of the cliffs began to move.

Huge boulders rolled down the hills, knocking the machines down into the pit.

"Why didn't you tell us you could do that before, Doctor Rock?" Wind asked.

"I couldn't do that until the liquid iron had been returned."

"Why?" Hydro looked puzzled.

"Last year I was experimenting with liquid iron in my lab and I accidentally came into contact with it. I cannot explain how I survived. From then I could use the power of liquid iron. But the levels were low so the power had no effect ... until now."

"I guess it really was a group effort, saving the world," Solar laughed.

The four returned to the Spy Control Centre. A note shone on the computer screen.

ALERT UPDATE: CODE STW

CURRENT STATUS: Liquid iron restored

RESULT: Day and night returned to both sides of the world

YOUR MISSION: Successful

Report to Energy Station One immediately.

You have saved the world.

Ms X